BLETCHLEY
TO
CAMBRIDGE

Vic Mitchell and Keith Smith

MP Middleton Press

Front Cover: The push-pull train from Bedford stands at Bletchley on 10th April 1948. LMS 0-4-4T no. 295 takes water after setting back from the centre of the platform. (H.C.Casserley)

Back Cover: The single car in NSE colours is towing one still in BR green and is seen at Millbrook in about 1997. A set of steps (left) compensated for the low height of the platform. (D.Lovett)

Published February 2007

ISBN   1 904474 94 2
*   978 1 904474 94 4*

© Middleton Press, 2007

Design Deborah Esher
Typesetting Barbara Mitchell

Published by
          Middleton Press
          Easebourne Lane
          Midhurst
          West Sussex
          GU29 9AZ
Tel: 01730 813169
Fax: 01730 812601
Email: info@middletonpress.co.uk
www.middletonpress.co.uk

Printed & bound by Biddles Ltd, Kings Lynn

INDEX

ACKNOWLEDGEMENTS

We are very grateful for the assistance received from many of those mentioned in the credits also to M.Burgoyne, A.R.Carder, P.Chancellor, G.Croughton, T.Heavyside, B.S.Jennings, J.Langford, N.Langridge, B.W.Leslie, D.Mitchell, Mr D. and Dr S.Salter, M.J.Stretton and particularly our ever supportive wives, Barbara Mitchell and Janet Smith.

I. The Railway Clearing House map of 1947 excluded all the 1905 halts.

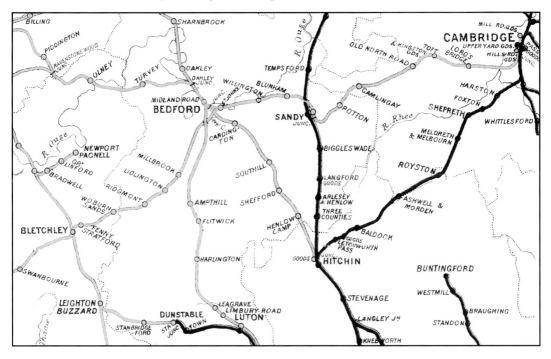

GEOGRAPHICAL SETTING

The Bletchley - Bedford section was built largely on Oxford Clay, which was of economic importance for brick making. The area is known as Marston Vale. Bedford is situated at the southern end of a ridge of Oolitic Limestone projecting south from the main mass which forms the extension northeast of the Cotswolds to Lincolnshire. The River Ouse flows round the west and south of the centre of the historic county town and the route follows the flow eastwards for about four miles.

At Sandy, the line reaches an obvious outcrop of Lower Greensand and continues to Cambridge close to the Gault Clay and Upper Greensand, which run parallel to and below the Chalk. This forms the northern extension of the Chiltern Hills in this vicinity. The east flowing Bourne Brook is followed closely for about six miles, before the route turns north; so does the water as it flows into the River Cam. This gives its name to the historic university city and commercial centre.

The first 4½ miles of the journey are in Buckinghamshire and the final 16 are in Cambridgeshire. The main part crosses Bedfordshire.

The maps are to the scale of 25ins to 1 mile, with north at the top, unless otherwise indicated.

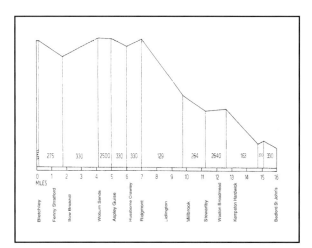

Gradient profile - Bletchley to Bedford

Gradient profile - Bedford to Cambridge. Only selected figures are shown due to the frequency of the changes, this being due to economical construction methods.

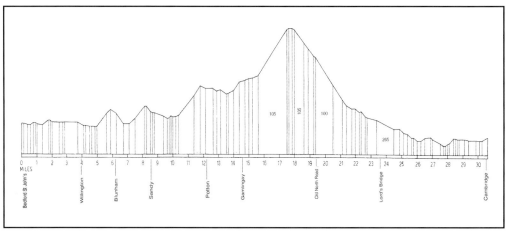

HISTORICAL BACKGROUND

We look at the lines radiating from London first, the termini there being shown in brackets.

The London & Birmingham Railway was completed through Bletchley in 1838 and it became part of the London & North Western Railway in 1846. (Euston)

The Midland Railway was opened through Bedford in 1857, but its trains ran via Hitchin, south of which they used the Great Northern Railway. The MR's own line between Bedford and London came into use in 1867. (St. Pancras)

The GNR was opened between Kings Cross and Peterborough in 1850, being crossed by our route at Sandy from 1862. (King's Cross, from 1852)

The Eastern Counties Railway reached Cambridge from London in 1845, it becoming a constituent of the Great Eastern Railway in 1862. (Liverpool Street)

It was on this network of four trunk routes that the Bletchley-Cambridge line was eventually superimposed. Bletchley received the Bedford Railway on 18th November 1846, its Act having been passed in 1845. It was Bedford's first railway. A line came from near Oxford to join it in 1850; this was owned by the Buckinghamshire Railway. Both railways became a branch of the LNWR.

The Sandy & Potton Railway was next on the scene, this opening on 9th December 1857 (or possibly 23rd June 1857). It was built on private land. An Act of Parliament on 6th August 1860 authorised the Bedford & Cambridge Railway, this incorporating the S&PR. The route opened on 1st August 1862. The B&CR became part of the LNWR in 1864 and the Bedford Railway followed in 1878, having been leased until that time.

The LNWR became a constituent of the London Midland & Scottish Railway in 1923 and this formed the London Midland Region of British Railways in England in 1948. However, the Willington - Cambridge section was transferred to the Eastern Region on 1st February 1958.

The route between Bedford and Cambridge closed completely on 1st January 1968, except the western two miles which carried power station coal until 1981. The Bletchley - Bedford section remains open to all traffic, due to the efforts of the Bedford & Bletchley Rail Users Association. The closures of individual goods yards are detailed in the captions.

The route came into the Northern Division of Network SouthEast on 10th June 1986. It became part of the North London Railways operating division of BR on 1st April 1984.

Privatisation of passenger services took place on 2nd March 1997, when Silverlink Train Services Ltd was awarded a 7½ year franchise; this was later extended by two years.

The Marston Vale Line (so named in 1995) was closed for six weeks in 2004 for installation of electric signalling and barriers at level crossings. It reopened on 6th September, with a signalling centre at Ridgmont.

PASSENGER SERVICES

The table below gives the number of down trains between the places shown, in selected years. Steam railcars (known as "Motors") were introduced in 1905 and diesel railcars came in 1959, although the first and last trains each day were locomotive-hauled for some years. Two or three trains ran through from Oxford in most years between 1862 and 1967; these did not stop at all stations.

	Bletchley - Bedford		Bedford - Cambridge	
	Weekdays	Sundays	Weekdays	Sundays
1846	5	2	-	-
1855	4	1	-	-
1864	6	1	5	1
1887	7	1	5	1
1908	12	1	6	1
1924	13	2	6	2
1939	13	6	6	4
1951	12	3	5	2
1964	17	0	9	0
1967	17	0	7	0
1987	15	0	-	-
2007	16	0	-	-

Sunday trains were withdrawn in 1963.

February 1887

Oxford and Bletchley to Cambridge

			SX	SO			SX	SO		SO	SO	SX	SO
OXFORD	d		06 24	07 53		09 44		11 30					13 15
ISLIP	d		06 37	08 07		09 57		11 44					13 26
BICESTER LONDON ROAD	d		06 46	08 17		10 06		11 53					13 35
LAUNTON	d		06 50	08 21				11 57					
MARSH GIBBON AND POUNDON	d		06 54	08 24				12 01					
CLAYDON	d		07 02	08 31				12 08					
VERNEY JUNCTION	d		07 06	08 36				12 12					
WINSLOW	d		07 11	08 41				12 17					
SWANBOURNE	d		07 15	08 46				12 21					
BLETCHLEY	a		07 25	08 55		10 36		12 31					
BLETCHLEY	d	06 35 07 14	08 08	09 08 09 25 09 25	10 38 11 25	12 07 12 15	13 10 13 42 14 00 14 50	15 10					
FENNY STRATFORD	d	06 37 07 16	08 10	09 10 09 27 09 27	11 27	12 09 12 17	13 12 13 44 14 02 14 52	15 12					
BOW BRICKHILL	d		08 13	09 30 09 30	11 30		13 15 13 47 14 55	15 15					
WOBURN SANDS	d	06 42 07 21	08 18	09 15 09 35 09 35	11 35	12 14 12 22	13 20 13 52 14 07 15 00	15 20					
ASPLEY GUISE	d	06 45	08 21	09 38 09 38	11 38		13 23 13 55 15 03	15 23					
RIDGMONT	d	06 49 07 26	08 25	09 20 09 42 09 42	11 42	12 19 12 27	13 27 13 59 14 12 15 07	15 27					
LIDLINGTON	d	06 53 07 30	08 29	09 24 09 46 09 46	11 46	12 23 12 31	13 31 14 03 14 16 15 11	15 31					
MILLBROOK	d	06 56 07 33	08 32	09 27 09 49 09 49	11 49	12 26 12 34	13 34 14 06 14 19 15 14	15 34					
STEWARTBY	d	06 59 07 36	08 35	09 30 09 52 09 52	11 52	12 29 12 37	13 37 14 09 14 22 15 17	15 37					
KEMPSTON HARDWICK	d	07 03	08 39	09 56 09 56	11 56		13 41 14 13 15 21	15 41					
BEDFORD ST. JOHN'S	a	07 09 07 44	08 45	09 38 10 02 10 58 12 02		12 37 12 45	13 47 14 19 14 30 15 27	15 47					
WILLINGTON	d	07 46	09 39	10 03 10 59		12 38 12 46	14 34						
BLUNHAM	d	07 54	09 48	10 11		12 47 12 55	14 43						
SANDY	d	07 59	09 53	10 16 11e14		12 52 13 00	14f52						
POTTON	d	08 04	09 58	10 21		12 57 13 05	14 57						
GAMLINGAY	d	08 10	10 04	10 27		13 03 13 11	15 03						
OLD NORTH ROAD	d	08 15	10 08	10 32		13 07 13 15	15 08						
LORD'S BRIDGE	d	08 23	10 16	10 40		13 15 13 23	15 16						
CAMBRIDGE	a	08 30	10 24	10 47		13 23 13 31	15 23						
CAMBRIDGE	a	08 41	10 31	10 56 11 43		13 33 13 40	15 33						

		SX	SX		SX	SO		❷	SO	SX	SX	SO	
[O]XFORD	d	14 32		17 18			18 48	19 53		22 50	22 55		
[ISLI]P	d	14 45		17 31			19 01				23 08		
[BIC]ESTER LONDON ROAD	d	14 53		17 41			19 11	20 14		23 11	23 20		
[LAU]NTON	d	14 58		17 45			19 15			23 15	23 24		
[MA]RSH GIBBON AND POUNDON	d	15 03		17 49			19 19				23 28		
[CLA]YDON	d	15 09		17 56			19 26			23 24	23 35		
[VER]NEY JUNCTION	d	15 13		18 00			19 30						
[WI]NSLOW	d	15 18		18 05			19 35			23 31	23 42		
[SW]ANBOURNE	d	15 23		18 09			19 39			23 36	23 46		
[BL]ETCHLEY	a	15 31		18 19			19 54	20 35		23 45	23 56		
[BL]ETCHLEY	d	15 53	16 22	17 11 17 38 18 15	18 53 18 46	19 54		20 53 20 53					
[FEN]NY STRATFORD	d	15 55	16 24	17 13 17 40 18 17	18 55 18 48			20 56 20 56					
[BO]W BRICKHILL	d		16 27	17 16 18 20	18 59 18 5L								
[WO]BURN SANDS	d	16 00	16 32	17 21 17 45 18 25	19 03 18 56			21 02 21 02					
[ASP]LEY GUISE	d		16 35	17 24 18 28	19 06 18 59								
[RID]GMONT	d	16 05	16 39	17 28 17 50 18a32	19 10 19 03			21 07 21 07					
[LID]LINGTON	d	16 09	16 43	17 32 17 54	19 14 19 07			21 11 21 11					
[MIL]LBROOK	d	16 12	16 46	17 35 17 57	19 17 19 10			21 14 21 14					
[STE]WARTBY	d		16 49	17 38 18 00	19 20 19 13								
[KEM]PSTON HARDWICK	d		16 53	17 42	19 24 19 17								
[BE]DFORD ST. JOHN'S	a	16 21	16 59	17 52 18 08	19 30 19 23	20 14		21 24 21 24					
[BE]DFORD ST. JOHN'S	d	16 25		17 57		19 23	20 15		21 26 21 26					
[WI]LLINGTON	d	16 33		18 01		19c36			21 34 21h40					
[BLUN]HAM	d	16 38		18 06		19 41			21 39 21 45					
[SAN]DY	d	16 45		18b17 18 23		19 46			21 44 21 50					
[POT]TON	d	16 51		18 27		19 52			21 50 21 56					
[GA]MLINGAY	d	16 55		18 35		19 57			21 55 22 01					
[OLD] NORTH ROAD	d	17 03		18 43					22 03 22 09					
[LOR]D'S BRIDGE	d	17 11												
[CA]MBRIDGE	a	17 21		18 50		20 18	20 56		22 19 22 25					

a Arrival time
b Arr 18 11
c Arr 19 32
e Arr 11 10
f Arr 14 48
h Arr 21 34

Final through timetable, issued April 1966.
SX Saturdays excepted
SO Saturdays only

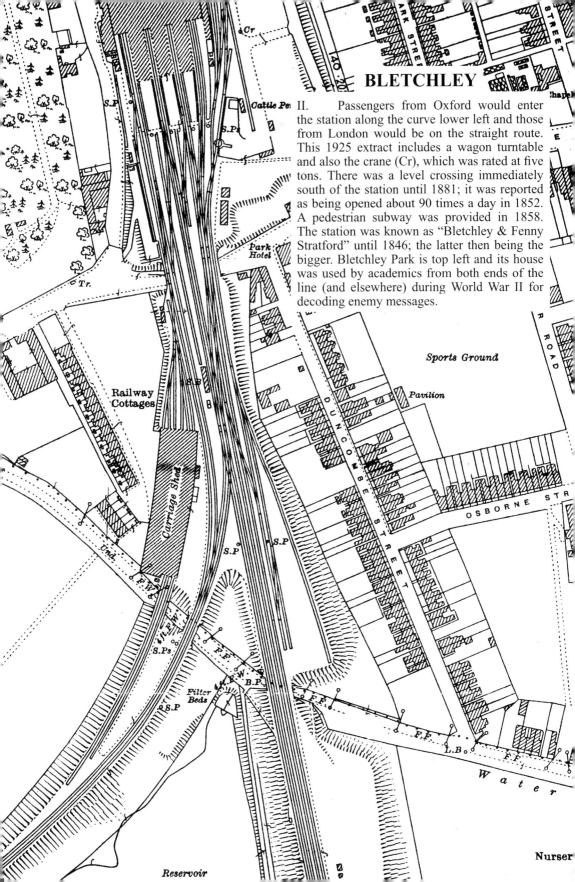

BLETCHLEY

II.   Passengers from Oxford would enter the station along the curve lower left and those from London would be on the straight route. This 1925 extract includes a wagon turntable and also the crane (Cr), which was rated at five tons. There was a level crossing immediately south of the station until 1881; it was reported as being opened about 90 times a day in 1852. A pedestrian subway was provided in 1858. The station was known as "Bletchley & Fenny Stratford" until 1846; the latter then being the bigger. Bletchley Park is top left and its house was used by academics from both ends of the line (and elsewhere) during World War II for decoding enemy messages.

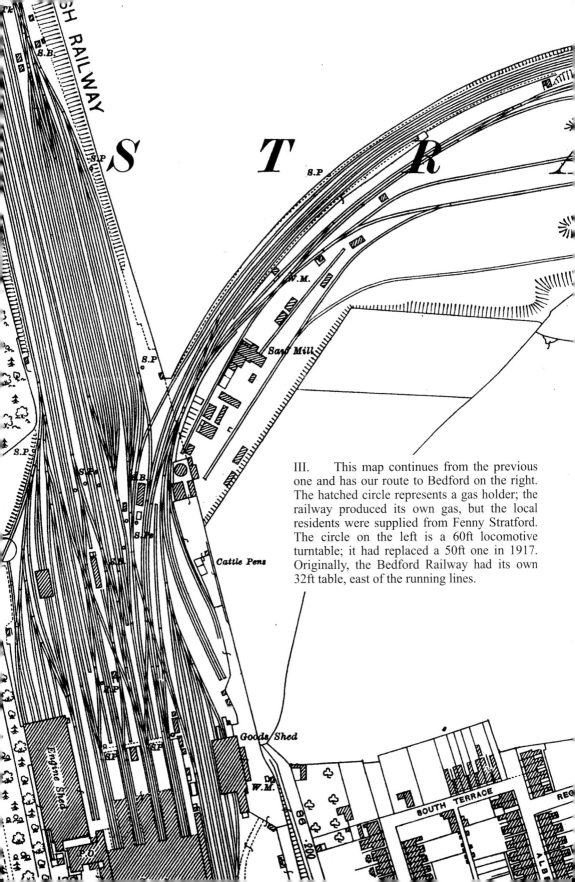

III. This map continues from the previous one and has our route to Bedford on the right. The hatched circle represents a gas holder; the railway produced its own gas, but the local residents were supplied from Fenny Stratford. The circle on the left is a 60ft locomotive turntable; it had replaced a 50ft one in 1917. Originally, the Bedford Railway had its own 32ft table, east of the running lines.

1.	The station shown on the maps, and also here, dates from the 1880 rebuild. This photograph is from 26th June 1920 and features 2-4-0 no. 477 *Caractacus* with a short train, probably from Bedford to Oxford. (R.S.Carpenter coll.)

2.	The engine shed was immediately northwest of the platforms and is seen on 29th January 1940, a hard time for the country in terms of both weather and war. The shed was coded 4A by BR and was 1E from 1959 until closure in July 1965. (H.C.Casserley)

3.   Class B12 4-6-0 no. 61558 is hauling a Cambridge-Oxford through train on 14th March 1957. Enjoy the fine architectural detailing, including a bay window on the stationmasters office. (P.Q.Treloar)

4.   The splendid entrance colonnade was recorded on 9th November 1963; this is also the date of the next four pictures. The Station Hotel is on the right, but all was soon to be destroyed. (J.C.Gillham)

5.	This southward view has platform 3 (down fast) on the right and 4 (up fast) on the left. In the distance is the flyover, which opened in January 1962; it was mainly for cross-country traffic, but was relatively little used and was closed for many years. A new use was found in 2006 in connection with the new Stewartby stone train operation. (J.C.Gillham)

6.	Trains from Bedford arrived at platform 8 (right), after passing the 80-lever No. 5 Box, which closed on 27th June 1965. No. 2 Box is centre and evidence of the loco shed is on the left. (J.C.Gillham)

7.   A northward panorama features No. 2 Box, which had 68 levers and controlled the line
north to No. 3 Box. On the right is No. 5 which is adjacent to the 20-chain curve for trains to
Bedford. The inclined embankment to the flyover is in the right background. The breakdown train
(left) included a 10-ton crane. No. 4 Box was at the east end of the Cambridge Sidings.
(J.C.Gillham)

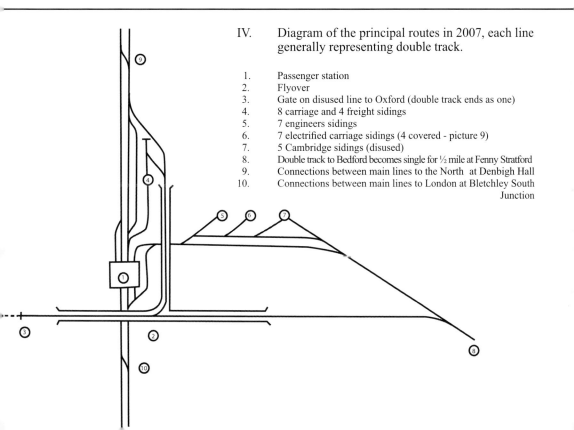

IV.   Diagram of the principal routes in 2007, each line
generally representing double track.

1.   Passenger station
2.   Flyover
3.   Gate on disused line to Oxford (double track ends as one)
4.   8 carriage and 4 freight sidings
5.   7 engineers sidings
6.   7 electrified carriage sidings (4 covered - picture 9)
7.   5 Cambridge sidings (disused)
8.   Double track to Bedford becomes single for ½ mile at Fenny Stratford
9.   Connections between main lines to the North at Denbigh Hall
10.   Connections between main lines to London at Bletchley South
                                                                                        Junction

8. This is the view from the former main entrance on platform 1 as rebuilding began prior to electrification. Part of platform 2 was retained, mainly for Buckingham trains until they were withdrawn in September 1964. More of the new flyover can be seen in the background; double tracks from the north and from the east converge on it, east of the station. (J.C.Gillham)

9. Electrification of the main lines was completed in April 1966 and a depot was built north of the Bedford line and east of the flyover embankment. The class 08 shunter is seen inside it in 1977. North of the curve are other sidings - see diagram IV. (D.Lovett)

10.   Following the rebuilding of the station, most Bedford trains have used the eastern (No. 6) platform, which retained its 1880s building, but not its canopy. Class 121 no. 55023 is working the 10.50 to Bedford on 6th May 1995. Platform numbers were altered after the rebuilding. (P.G.Barnes)

11.   On 23rd April 1999, the short lived formation of two class 31s with two coaches was recorded. Nearest is no. 31452; at the other end is no. 31468. New lifts were provided in 2003, but there was still not one at platform 6. Trains carrying wheelchairs would be diverted to No. 5. The old platform building was demolished in 1999. (P.Jones)

The construction of the flyover and other aspects of the station are illustrated in our *Oxford to Bletchley* album.

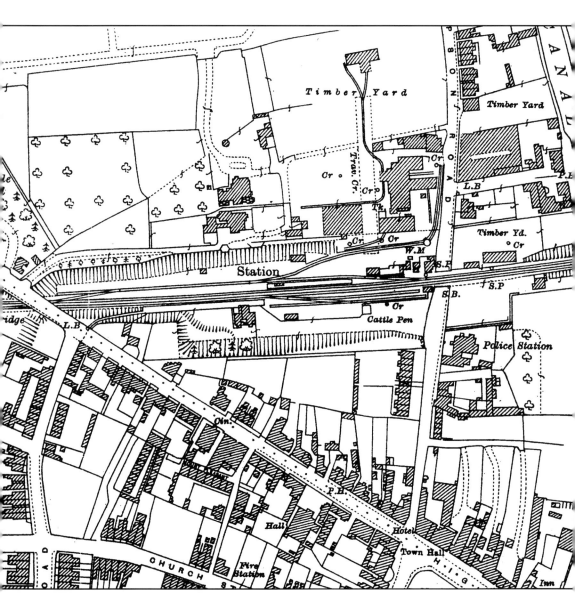

V.   The 1925 map includes the awkwardly abbreviated Grand Junction Canal on the right. The Fenny Stratford Gas Company of 1857 obtained its coal initially by barge. By 1900, its own wagons were conveying 684 tons by rail, this figure rising to 4600 tons by 1947. Traffic ceased with the advent of a gas grid in 1957. The goods yard crane was rated at three tons; it is near the cattle pen.

12.   The population was under 700 when the railway arrived, 3571 in 1901 and over 6000 in 1961. This view east is from an early postcard and includes the crane in Rowland's timber yard. The platforms were staggered. (Lens of Sutton coll.)

13.   The platform on the left was built in 1948, but still no footbridge was provided. The inclined path to the up platform is on the right in this 1954 photograph. (British Railways)

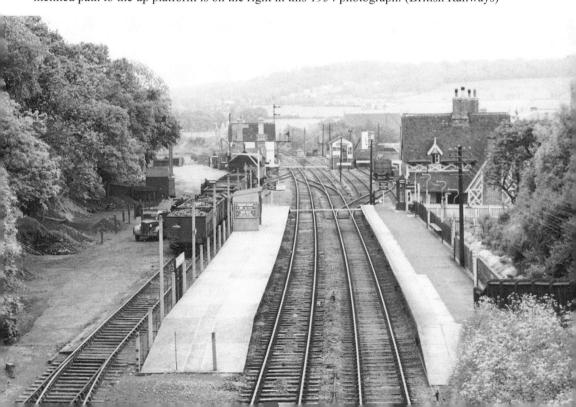

14.   The 1948 platform is seen from an up train in June 1955, with a much repaired wagon nearest. On the extreme right is Rowland's siding, which came into use in October 1882. The bridge carried the A5 Watling Street. (Millbrook House)

←
15.   An eastward view in February 1966 includes the gas holder and the southern part of the goods yard. Local freight traffic ceased on 22nd May 1967 and staffing ended on 15th July 1968. (E.Wilmshurst)

16.   The line through the station was singled in 1972, but the elegant building remained intact. The 1948 platform was dismantled for reuse at Bedford in 1984. (British Railways)

17.   Looking west under Watling Street, we see the flyover line curving from the original route, which turns to the right first. Both are single for a short distance. Electric lighting dates from 1948. The platform takes four coaches. (D.Lovett)

18.   A view in the other direction on 5th May 1999 contains mechanical signalling and the train seen in picture 11. It is passing over the level crossing evident in No. 12. (C.G.Maggs)

19.   The level crossing at Simpson Road was controlled by this box from about 1884 until 2004.
Full lifting barriers replaced the gates. The site between here and the station was redeveloped in
2005-6 and a fenced path provided. (D.Lovett)

BOW BRICKHILL

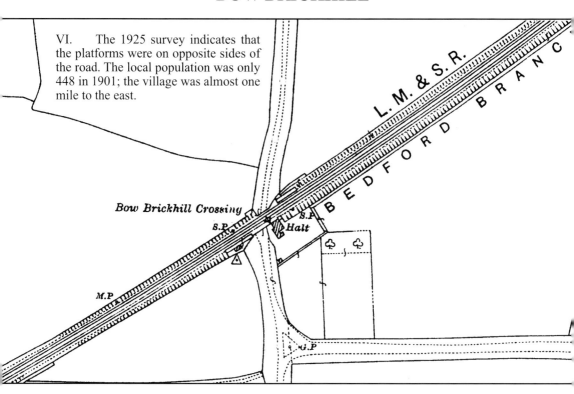

VI.   The 1925 survey indicates that the platforms were on opposite sides of the road. The local population was only 448 in 1901; the village was almost one mile to the east.

20.   Looking towards Bletchley in July 1959, we examine the first of the ground level halts on our journey. It opened on 30th October 1905 and was closed between 1st January 1917 and 5th May 1919, due to World War I. (H.C.Casserley)

21.   A view in the other direction includes the crossing keepers accommodation, which was probably built with the line. The signal box had four levers in use, but no gate wheel. (R.M.Casserley)

0076   0076   0076

7 | 8 | 9 | 10 | 6 | 8 | 7
British Railways Board (M) 1402
BOW BRICKHILL
PLATFORM TICKET
Not valid in Trains   Not Transferable
Issued to Commemorate the
140th Anniversary of the
Bletchley—Bedford Line 1846—1986
This ticket may be retained as a souvenir
1 | 2 | 3 | 4 | 5 | 6

2690   2690   2690

2nd - SINGLE   SINGLE - 2nd

Woburn Sands to

Woburn Sands   Woburn Sands
Bow Brickhill   Bow Brickhill

BOW BRICKHILL

(M)   0/9   Fare   0/9   (M)
For conditions see over   For conditions see over

22.　　A two-car class 104 DMU approaches the down platform on 2nd June 1984. Both were designed for just two coaches. Lifting barriers came later. (M.Turvey)

23.　　Both platforms had been raised to standard height in 1959. This is the up one in August 1998, but it retained a lower level waiting shelter. (C.G.Maggs)

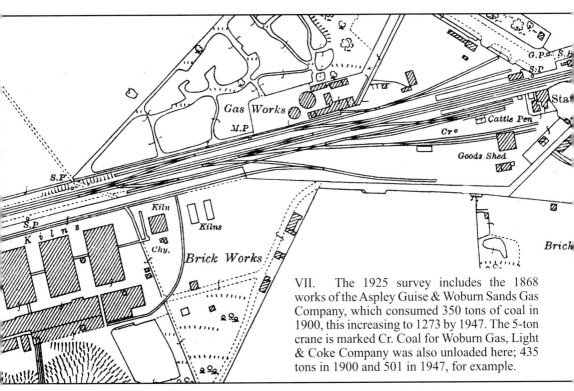

VII.   The 1925 survey includes the 1868 works of the Aspley Guise & Woburn Sands Gas Company, which consumed 350 tons of coal in 1900, this increasing to 1273 by 1947. The 5-ton crane is marked Cr. Coal for Woburn Gas, Light & Coke Company was also unloaded here; 435 tons in 1900 and 501 in 1947, for example.

24.   The station was initially simply "Woburn", although the district had earlier been known as Hogsty End. "Sands" was added in 1860; brickmaking was already well established by that time. An early engraving suggests a low timber platform with rather prominent scales. (C.G.Maggs coll.)

25.   Photographs of the LNWR railmotors are rare, as they were replaced by push-pull trains by 1926. This example is at the down platform, some while after their introduction in 1905. (Lens of Sutton coll.)

26.   A splendid Edwardian record includes the scales shelter and the signal box, which was fitted with a gate wheel and 27 levers. (Lens of Sutton coll.)

27. This is the south side of the station in July 1958; a few horse-drawn carts lasted into the 1960s. On the left is the entrance to the goods yard, which had a five-ton crane. It is shown on the map. The population was 1381 in 1961. (R.M.Casserley)

28. Goods facilities were withdrawn on 22nd May 1967. Seen in 1978, the coal yard was in commercial use and the gasworks was still standing. (D.Lovett)

29.   The generous proportions of the down side shelter are revealed in this view from January 1993. The signal box lasted until 24th July 2004. The ornate buildings had been demanded by the Duke of Bedford, as a condition of the sale of the land. (D.Trevor Rowe)

30.   By the time that this photograph was taken on 2nd August 1998, the building had been listed Grade II. Both platforms took three coaches, at this time. (C.G.Maggs)

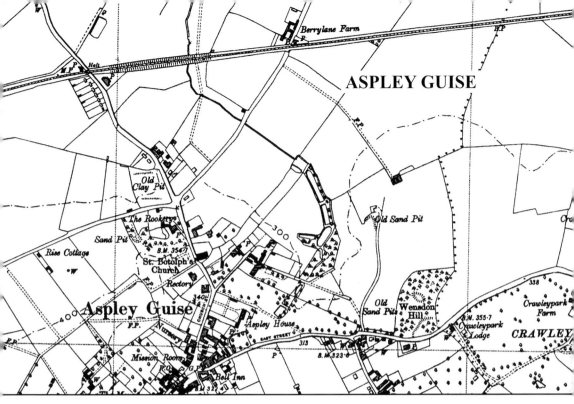

VIII.   The 1952 survey at 6ins to 1 mile indicates the proximity of the halt to the village, which had 1921 residents in 1961. The opening dates are as in caption 20. The crossing near Berrylane Farm had an attendant until 1967.

31.   No. 55031 was working the 10.40 from Bedford on 6th May 1995. Each platform would accommodate two coaches. Husborne Crawley was once the next stop east; its dates were the same, but it closed on 5th May 1941, permanently. (P.G.Barnes)

32.   Moments later the unit departs for Bletchley and the gates are opened for road traffic. For many years, the reverse applied and road users had to ring a bell for the gates to be opened, when safe to do so. Full barriers with CCTV came into use on 6th September 2004. (P.G.Barnes)

33.   The 150th anniversary of the opening of the route was celebrated on 21st December 1996 with some steam hauled specials. BR class 4MT 2-6-4T no. 80079 was normally based at the Severn Valley Railway. (M.Turvey)

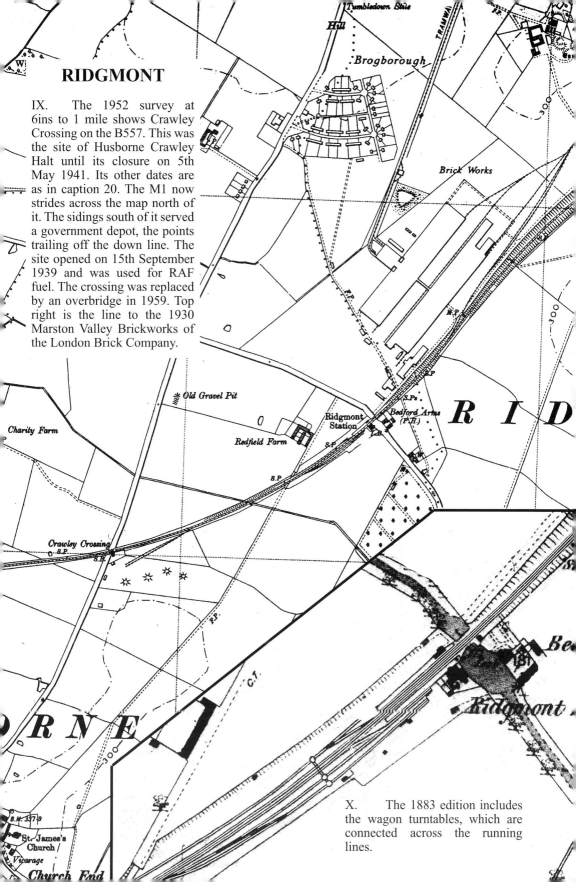

RIDGMONT

IX. The 1952 survey at 6ins to 1 mile shows Crawley Crossing on the B557. This was the site of Husborne Crawley Halt until its closure on 5th May 1941. Its other dates are as in caption 20. The M1 now strides across the map north of it. The sidings south of it served a government depot, the points trailing off the down line. The site opened on 15th September 1939 and was used for RAF fuel. The crossing was replaced by an overbridge in 1959. Top right is the line to the 1930 Marston Valley Brickworks of the London Brick Company.

X. The 1883 edition includes the wagon turntables, which are connected across the running lines.

34.   An eastward view from 1917 includes the Bedford Arms, one of few buildings in the vicinity at that time. The symmetry of the porches and the massive coping stones of the platform are worthy of note. (R.S.Carpenter coll.)

35.   The new M1 bridge is in the background, above the 1934 Hillman 10. The goods yard is between them; it closed on 3rd August 1964. (H.C.Casserley)

36.   The village is one mile southeast of the station. It had 591 residents in 1901 and 808 in 1961. The intricate barge boards and most of the ornamental framing could still be admired in September 1967. (R.M.Casserley)

37.   The 13-lever frame (right) was situated in a signal box on the other side of the road until 1934. It was moved here so that one man could issue tickets and operate it; he also had to work the gates. It was a block post and there was a ground frame at the far end of the brickworks loop. The box under the lamp housed six intruments and seven plungers and is seen in 1985. (P.G.Barnes)

38.   Colour light signals and barriers with CCTV became operational on 6th September 2004. New coping slabs, waiting shelters and Sprinter no. 150127 are seen on 5th May 2006. Both platforms will take three-car units. The Marston Vale Signalling Control Centre was established here in 2004; it is just beyond the left border of the picture. (M.Turvey)

LIDLINGTON

XI.   The 1925 edition shows habitation nearby. The station is close to the village, which housed
515 souls in 1901. There were no goods facilities here.

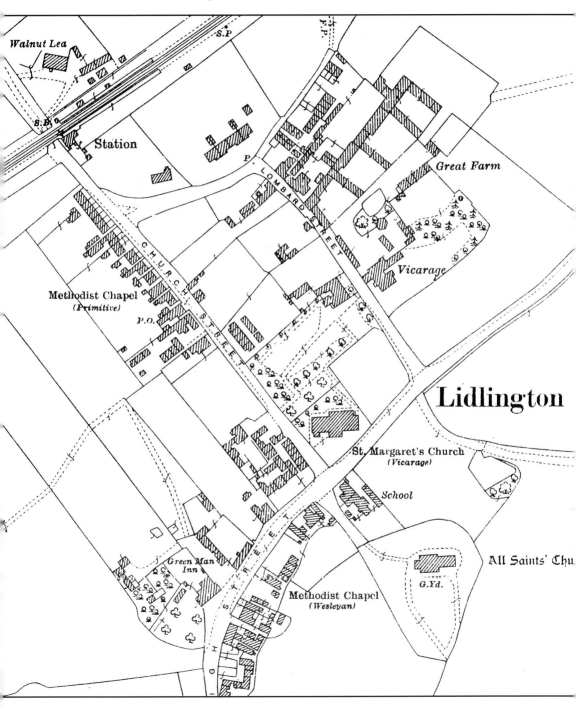

39.		The west elevation was recorded in 1967, the year in which staffing ceased. The design is that used at crossings and is thus unique as a station building on the route. (R.M.Casserley)

40.		On the left is the crossing keepers hut, which has an external four-lever frame. It was not a block post. Note the different levels of the up platform in this August 1992 view. Both could take three coaches. (D.Trevor Rowe)

41. The gate man is at his levers as the 11.50 from Bletchley approaches on 12th October 1996. The train is formed of two class 121 units, known by many as "Bubblecars", a term used in the 1950s for small cars. (P.G.Barnes)

42. A closer look at the frame and hut includes the path used by all down platform passengers. The levers control two signals in each direction to protect the gates. All vanished in August 2004 in favour of barriers with CCTV and a new up platform was built west of the road. (P.G.Barnes)

MILLBROOK

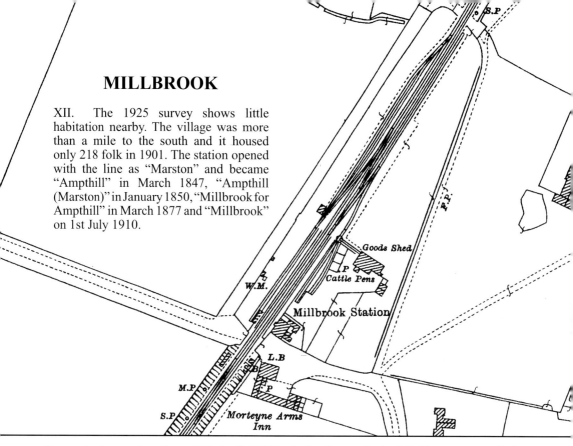

XII. The 1925 survey shows little habitation nearby. The village was more than a mile to the south and it housed only 218 folk in 1901. The station opened with the line as "Marston" and became "Ampthill" in March 1847, "Ampthill (Marston)" in January 1850, "Millbrook for Ampthill" in March 1877 and "Millbrook" on 1st July 1910.

Goods Shed

Cattle Pens

W.M.

Millbrook Station

L.B

M.P.

S.P.

Morteyne Arms Inn

43. A view eastwards on 13th April 1959 includes the goods shed (left), access to which was always by way of a wagon turntable - see map. Goods traffic ceased on 3rd August 1964. (R.M.Casserley)

44.   We have not examined the rear of a station building yet. This 1959 photograph shows the jetty under the first floor and that the out-buildings carried the same pitch roofs, albeit with simple barge boards. (R.M.Casserley)

45.   Here the lever frame was not moved to the platform, but was raised on to a stage outside the box. It gave good visibility and received the name "Millbrook Station". (E.Wilmshurst)

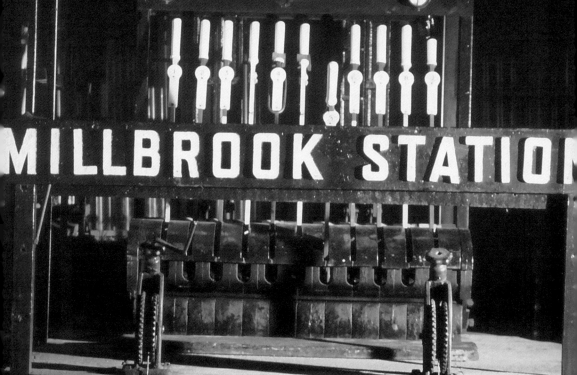

46.   A second photograph from February 1966 includes the up starting signal. This includes more of the spacious down waiting shelter, as a DMU arrives from Bletchley. Staffing ceased on 15th July 1968. (E.Wilmshurst)

47.   A close-up of Millbrook Station frame confirms its suitability for operation by staff suffering from claustrophobia. (D.Lovett)

48.   A class 105 DMU was restored to its original green livery and was photographed on 28th May 1988. The platform still retained its blue chequered Staffordshire paving bricks and the portable steps used by the less nimble passengers. (P.G.Barnes)

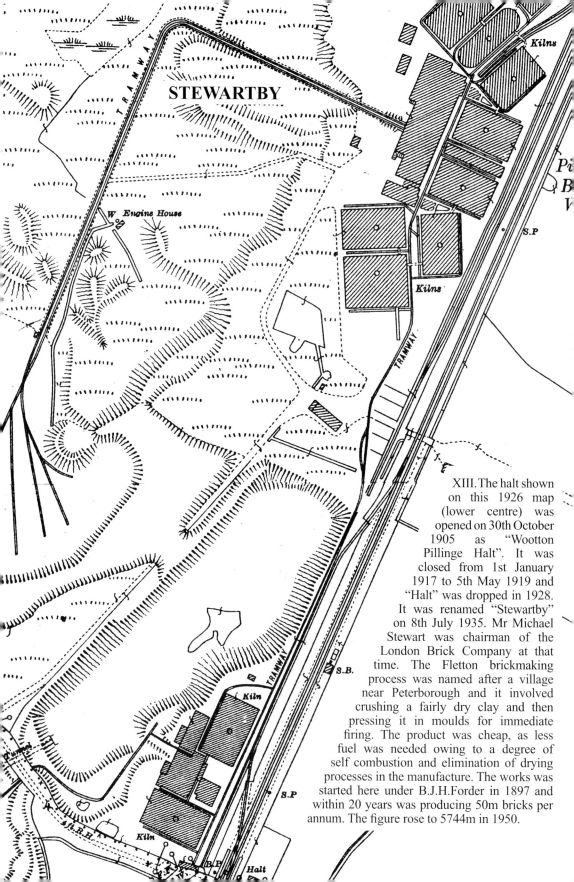

STEWARTBY

W Engine House

Kilns

Kilns

S.P.

TRAMWAY

TRAMWAY

S.B.

Kiln

S.P.

Kiln

Halt

XIII. The halt shown on this 1926 map (lower centre) was opened on 30th October 1905 as "Wootton Pillinge Halt". It was closed from 1st January 1917 to 5th May 1919 and "Halt" was dropped in 1928. It was renamed "Stewartby" on 8th July 1935. Mr Michael Stewart was chairman of the London Brick Company at that time. The Fletton brickmaking process was named after a village near Peterborough and it involved crushing a fairly dry clay and then pressing it in moulds for immediate firing. The product was cheap, as less fuel was needed owing to a degree of self combustion and elimination of drying processes in the manufacture. The works was started here under B.J.H.Forder in 1897 and within 20 years was producing 50m bricks per annum. The figure rose to 5744m in 1950.

49.   The profusion of chimneys gives an idea of the magnitude of the brick output. Note that oil lamps were still in use on 29th September 1967. This view is towards Bedford. (H.C.Casserley)

50.   Bound for Bletchley on 21st December 1996, this service was unusual in being formed of three coaches. The up platform was moved south of the level crossing in 2004; both were two-car lengths thereafter. Automatic half barriers were installed. (M.Turvey)

51.   Seen on the same day, no. 31420 approaches from the south prior to taking up shunting duties in Forders Sidings. Fletliner brick containers had been used in 1972-85, but all brick traffic ceased thereafter. (M.Turvey)

NORTH OF STEWARTBY

52.   London's rubbish began arriving in April 1974, as a landfill operation to restore the clay pit areas. It was soon coming at the rate of 1200 tons per day. One batch is seen behind no. 31294 on 4th September 1990. The gantry once used for brick containers was used for this traffic, but it came to an end in April 2005, when the landfill site was deemed full. It had been operated by Shanks and McEwan. This southward view has the 40-lever Forders Sidings box on the left and the small shunt signal is off, ready for the train to enter the bidirectional loop. The box was taken out of use on 24th July 2004, but was still standing at the end of 2006. (M.Turvey)

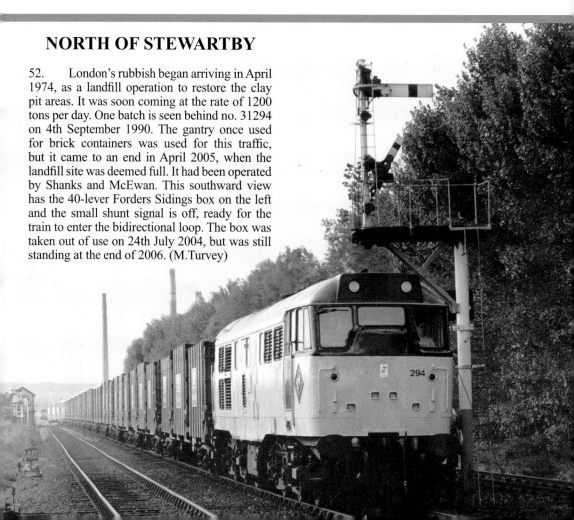

53.   Branching from the loop are two lines, the left one leads to 13 sidings near the centre of which is the massive ballast stockpile. Two class 66 diesels wait to leave and may run via Bedford or Bletchley. The line curving to the right serves six sidings, the first two passing under two travelling gantry cranes. Seen in December 2006, the virtual quarry had previously been at Rugby. (V.Mitchell)

WOOTTON BROADMEAD

54.   The dates for this halt were as for Husborne Crawley (caption 31). It was located near the north end of Forders Sidings. Only the crossing keepers house remained to be photographed on 29th September 1967 as no. D336 ran north. There are now full barriers with CCTV. (H.C.Casserley)

KEMPSTON HARDWICK

55.   Northbound on 1st May 1999 is the curious combination described in caption 11. The crossing is on a lane north from the village. Eastwoods Flettons Ltd had sidings east of the line from 1928. (M.Turvey)

56.   The crossing was fitted with automatic half barriers in 2004 and has one of the worst records for delinquent motorist abuse in the UK. No. 150123 is bound for Bletchley on 5th May 2006. Kempston & Elstow Halt was further north, close to the bridge under the MR. Its dates are as in caption 31. (M.Turvey)

BEDFORD ST. JOHNS

XIV.   The 1938 map at 6ins to 1 mile has the former MR main line close to the left border of the page, through lines bypassing the principal station. Our route is from the lower to the right border, it crossing over the Hitchin line on the level into St. Johns station.

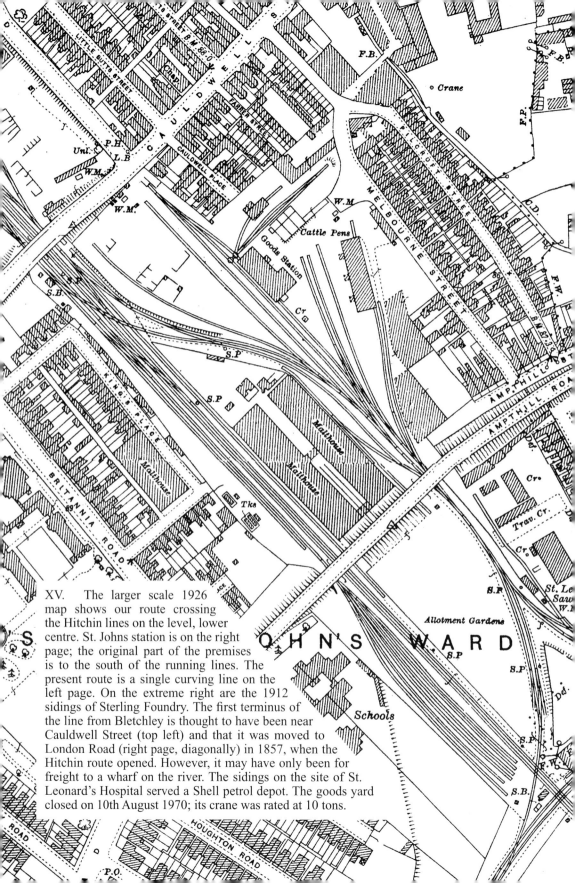

XV. The larger scale 1926 map shows our route crossing the Hitchin lines on the level, lower centre. St. Johns station is on the right page; the original part of the premises is to the south of the running lines. The present route is a single curving line on the left page. On the extreme right are the 1912 sidings of Sterling Foundry. The first terminus of the line from Bletchley is thought to have been near Cauldwell Street (top left) and that it was moved to London Road (right page, diagonally) in 1857, when the Hitchin route opened. However, it may have only been for freight to a wharf on the river. The sidings on the site of St. Leonard's Hospital served a Shell petrol depot. The goods yard closed on 10th August 1970; its crane was rated at 10 tons.

57.   We look west from London Road bridge in the mid-1870s. On the left is the Bedford Railway's terminus, which was later used for through trains. The engine shed is in the distance. (It closed in 1923.) The signal post was slotted, so that the arms were lowered inside it; the lamps were separate and lower down the post. (Railway Magazine)

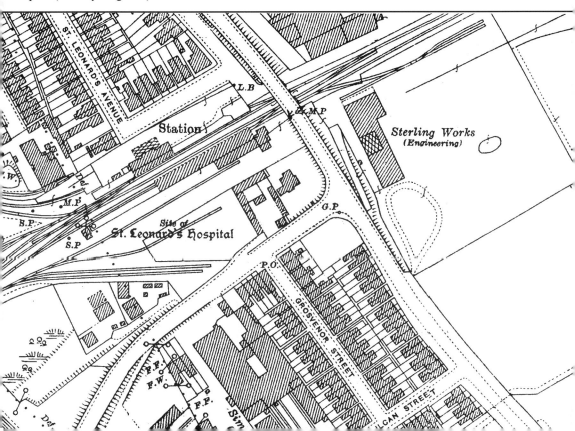

58.   The 1862 building was in extreme contrast, having a porte-cochère to protect those using road transport. This panorama is also from London Road, but in the Edwardian era. The suffix "St. Johns" was added in 1924. (Lens of Sutton coll.)

59.   The west ends of the two stations can be compared in this photograph from 7th November 1953. BR class 4 4-6-0 no. 75038 will soon move its train into the "London" platform (right) and leave for Bletchley at 4.20pm. (T.J.Edgington)

60.   No. 1 Box had 50 levers and the Hitchin lines cross our route on the level, right of centre. The curve on the left is treated similarly, beyond the edge of the picture. This line was used for freight only until 1984. St. Johns station and a horse box are in the distance. On the left is the massive flour mill. (D.Lawrence)

61.   A short parcel train from Cambridge is about to pass under London Road in about 1960. The locomotive is class 2MT 2-6-2T no. 42071. On the right is the gateway through which wagons once passed to the foundry. The bus garage was used successively by London General, United Counties and Stagecoach. (M.Turvey)

62.   A westward panorama of the desolate scene in October 1971 shows a train arriving from Bletchley, together with the Shell sidings on the left. Hidden by grass on the right is the curve that would take all trains from 1984. (T.J.Edgington)

63.   A DMU is signalled to leave the remains of the original terminus on 6th May 1981. It had become a terminus again in 1968. The building on the other platform had been demolished in 1971 and only a shunt signal remained on it. On the right is a flat-roofed signal box. This had replaced the one seen in picture 60 in about 1970, following a fire. The Hitchin line had lost its passenger trains in 1962 and closed to through freight in 1964. (B.Morrison)

64.	All FA Cup Final specials from Nottingham to Wembley travelled via Bedford, the Bletchley Flyover and High Wycombe on 18th May 1991. No. 47520 regains double track, having crept over the many curves down from the main line. The signal box is close to the Hitchin line trackbed and was a fringe box to West Hampstead. It was still standing in 2006, in ruins. (B.Morrison)

65.	Fenny Stratford down platform was re-erected near Ampthill Road and was opened on 14th May 1984 to replace the ones seen in picture 63. There were no objections to the closure of the old station and all trains ran to the former MR station thereafter. This view is from the north end of the platform on 2nd December 2006. (V.Mitchell)

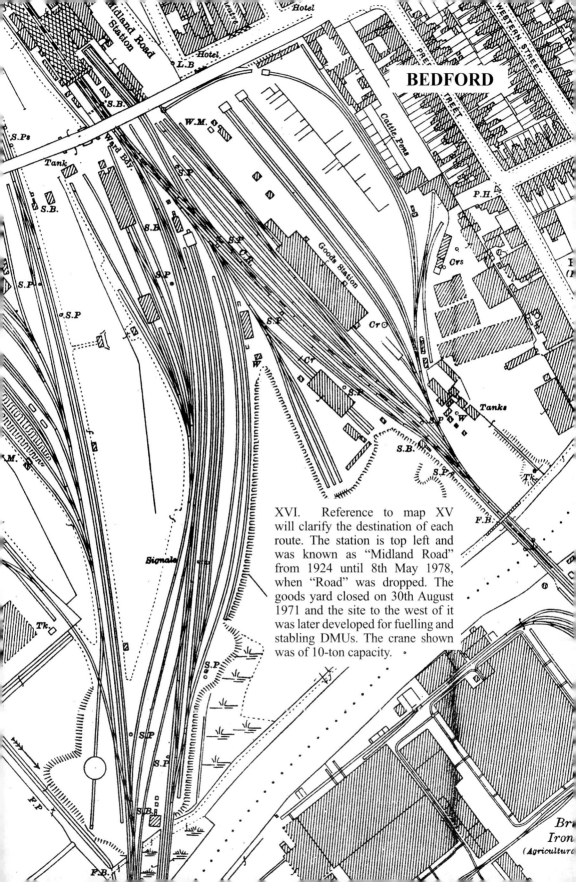

BEDFORD

XVI. Reference to map XV will clarify the destination of each route. The station is top left and was known as "Midland Road" from 1924 until 8th May 1978, when "Road" was dropped. The goods yard closed on 30th August 1971 and the site to the west of it was later developed for fuelling and stabling DMUs. The crane shown was of 10-ton capacity.

Other views of this station can be found in
***St. Albans to Bedford* and *Bedford to Wellingborough*.**

←———

66.   A new station was constructed slightly northwest of the original so that it could also serve the through lines. It is seen in 1980 with a DMU departing for St Pancras. It opened on 9th October 1978 and the suffix "Midland" was dropped on 5th May 1988. (M.Turvey)

←———

67.   This is the view south from the footbridge on the right of the last map on 28th May 1988, as class 4MT 2-6-4T no. 80080 uses the depot approach line for short trips on an Open Day. (P.G.Barnes)

68.   Turning round, we witness a then rare green liveried class 105 DMU running to Bletchley at 13.37. It is single line for one mile south from the station, which is just beyond the bridge in the background. The former goods yard found a new use with the engineers, but was little used in 2006, although the goods shed was still standing, stabling of tampers was the main use. (P.G.Barnes)

69.	The bay has been seen in the right of picture 66 and the bridge is in no. 68. This has been the end of the journey for most trains from Bletchley since 1984. Numbered 1a, the bay takes four cars, whereas the other four accommodate 11 or 12. The date is 6th May 1995 and the other platforms would soon be used by Midland Mainline and Thameslink. The latter meaningful title was changed to First Capital Connect in April 2006. (P.G.Barnes)

70.	Approaching platform 1a on 2nd December 2006 is "Sprinter" no. 150121 from Bletchley. The lines in the foreground are designated "Slow" and diverging from the up slow under the arch is the connection to the 14 sidings of the EMU depot. A further eight were provided south of the river in September 2004, four being under cover. The figure 64 refers to the radio communication area. (V.Mitchell)

EAST OF BEDFORD ST. JOHNS

71.　　Trains to Goldington Power Station used the line in the foreground of picture 63 until 1981. It came into use in 1948, its siding branching from a loop on the single line to Sandy. There was also one to Bedford Corporation's Newnham Depot. Bedford St. Johns No. 2 Box was at the end of the double track and was in use until 25th January 1970. The Andrew Barclay 0-4-0ST was no. ED9 *Matthew Murray* and was oil fired. Built in 1954, it was photographed on 9th November 1971. (Milepost 92½)

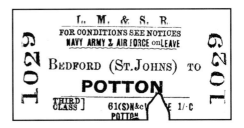

WILLINGTON

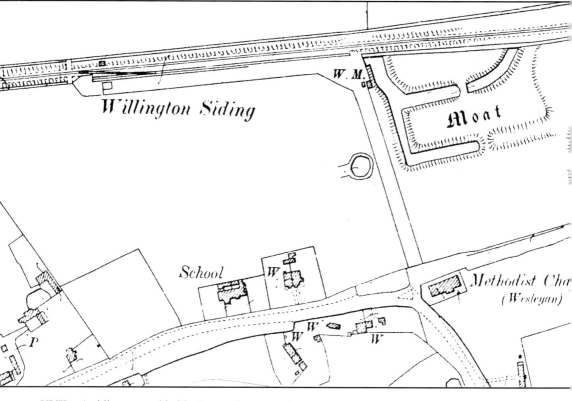

XVII. A siding was added in September 1896 for vegetable traffic in particular and it is seen on the 1900 edition, along with the location of the weighing machine (W.M.).

72.   A view towards Bedford includes an LMS style hawkseye sign and evidence of platform lengthening. The station opened on 1st May 1903 and is seen in about 1960. (Lens of Sutton)

73. The signal box had 20 levers and was at the east end of the down platform. The crossing is included in this 1967 view. The goods yard closed on 13th July 1964. (R.Hummerston)

XVIII. The 1926 survey includes only part of the lengthy passing loop on the single line to Sandy. The population rose from 204 in 1901 to 475 in 1961.

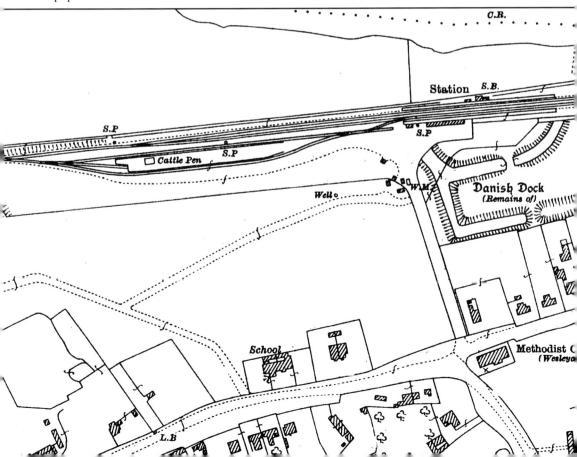

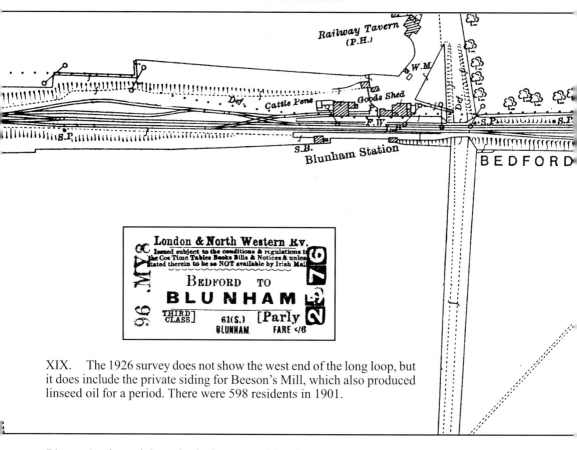

XIX. The 1926 survey does not show the west end of the long loop, but it does include the private siding for Beeson's Mill, which also produced linseed oil for a period. There were 598 residents in 1901.

74. A substantial goods shed was provided, but no footbridge was ever built here. The yard seems busy in this early postcard view. (Lens of Sutton coll.)

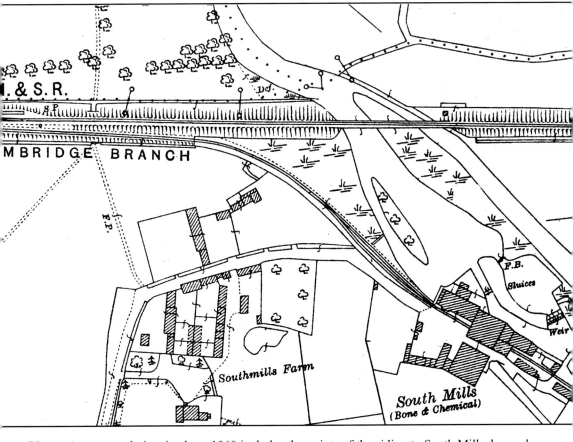

75.   An eastward view in about 1960 includes the points of the siding to South Mills, beyond
the road bridge. The single line sections were supplied with the electric train staff system in 1888,
one of the earliest such installations. (Lens of Sutton coll.)

76.   The shed contained a 25cwt crane and the signal box housed a 20-lever frame. Goods traffic ceased on 13th July 1964 and houses now occupy the station site. Next stop east was Girtford Halt, but it was only open from 1st January 1938 to 17th November 1940. However, there was an agricultural siding there from 1863 until 1951, on the north side of the line. (Lens of Sutton coll.)

77.   The up platform had been shortened by removal of the timber part prior to this view being taken on closing day. The structure on the right is the rodding tunnel. In the distance is the buffer stop at the end of the loop. (R.Hummerston)

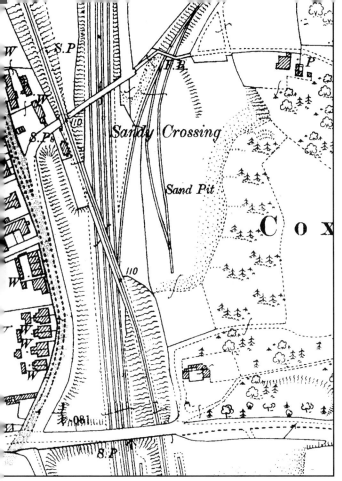

NORTH OF SANDY

XX. The 1901 survey has the LNWR single line from Bedford top left, the GNR quadruple track main line next and finally a siding to Sandy Brick & Tile Works. There are single sidings of both companies at the bottom. There was a north-west connection between the two routes for wartime traffic from September 1940. It was used by freight and irregularly by passengers until January 1961, when it became sidings. The curve was double track with Sandy North Junction on the LMS and Sandy LNE Junction (later Sandy West) at the other end. The ex-LNWR bridge span over the main line was renewed in 1956 and removed in 1975.

78.   This northward view is taken from a bridge beyond the lower border of the map and includes both sidings. No. 25319 is running towards Cambridge on 27th June 1936. (L.Hanson/P.Q.Treloar coll.)

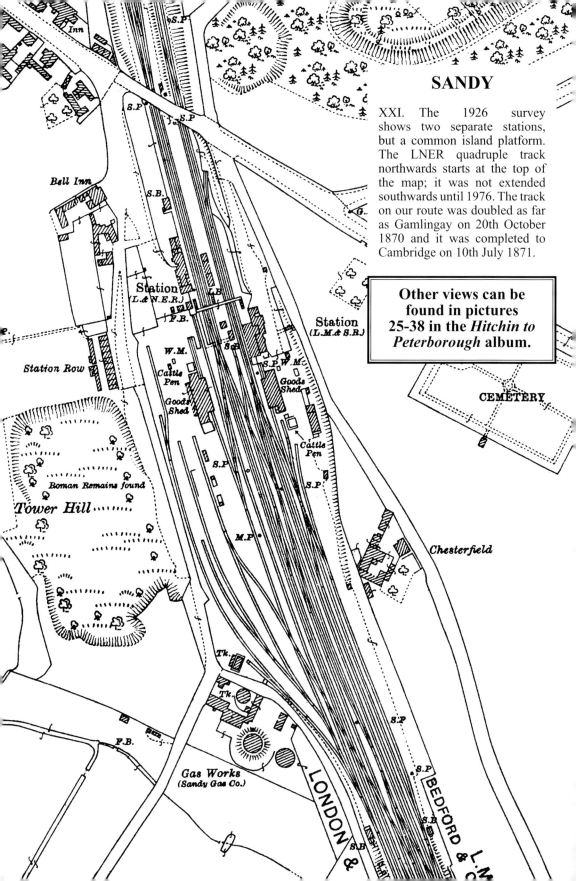

SANDY

XXI. The 1926 survey shows two separate stations, but a common island platform. The LNER quadruple track northwards starts at the top of the map; it was not extended southwards until 1976. The track on our route was doubled as far as Gamlingay on 20th October 1870 and it was completed to Cambridge on 10th July 1871.

Other views can be found in pictures 25-38 in the *Hitchin to Peterborough* album.

79.   A southward panorama from the bridge at the top of the map features the GNR platforms and its signal box, called Sandy North. No. 1416 was an "Atlantic" class C1 4-4-2, but sadly cropped by the photographer. (Lens of Sutton coll.)

80.   Climbing out of the station and bound for Bedford on 1st May 1937 is 2-6-4T no. 2600. The LNER up line is in the lower right corner. Like Exeter St. Davids, the other up trains ran in the opposite direction. (L.Hanson/P.Q.Treloar coll.)

81.   Southbound on the former LNER up line on 3rd March 1961 is ex-Ministry of Supply 2-8-0 no. 90180, formerly no. 77204. Its steam is obscuring the bridge span over the Bedford-Cambridge line. (Unknown)

82.   No. 1 Box is featured in this view of the last day of operation to Cambridge. It had a 30-lever frame and its companion (No. 2) is shown near the word BEDFORD at the bottom of the map. The exchange sidings were between the boxes. (R.Hummerston)

London & North Western Rv.
Issued subject to the conditions & regulations in the Cos Time Tables Books Bills & Notices.
BEDFORD   TO
SANDY (L.&N.W.)
(D)
Third]   61(S)   [Class
          SANDY   FARE -/8½

6895

83.   Looking north in July 1973, we observe that little had changed in six years, since the last train had left. The platforms were removed in 1975 to permit quadrupling of the main line, at last. (J.Mann/Ted Hancock)

POTTON

84.   The first trains to Potton were hauled by this 0-4-0WT, built by George England for the line in 1857. The Sandy & Potton Railway was constructed by Sir William Peel, a captain in the Royal Navy, and the locomotive was named *Shannon*, after one of his ships. When the engine became LNWR property, it was used in Crewe Works until sold to the Wantage Tramway in 1878. It is seen working the last passenger service on that line in 1925. Its subsequent survival to become a star at the Didcot Railway Centre is explained in captions in our *Branch Line to Wantage* album. (F.E.J.Burgiss coll.)

XXII.   The location of the S&PR terminus was the field at the bottom of the map opposite. This plan of 1856 has a line passing through the goods shed, the engine shed at the end of it and the station buildings above the latter. The usages are assumed, based on contemporary practices.

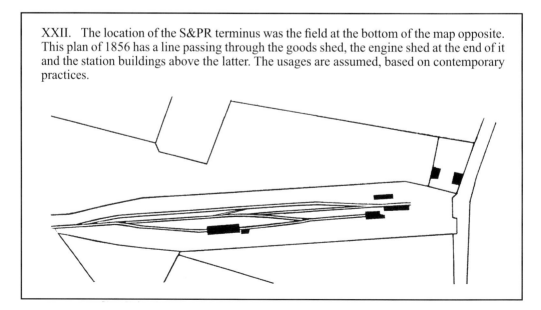

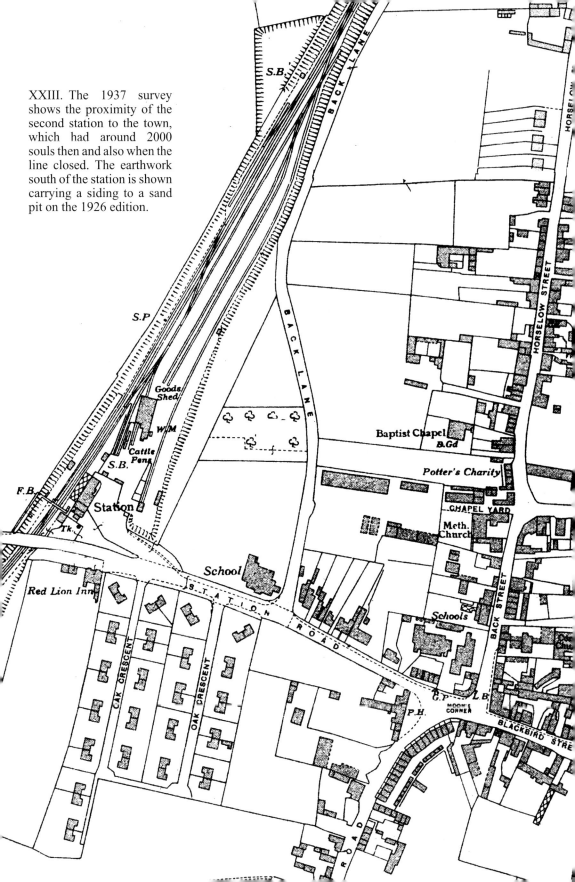

XXIII. The 1937 survey shows the proximity of the second station to the town, which had around 2000 souls then and also when the line closed. The earthwork south of the station is shown carrying a siding to a sand pit on the 1926 edition.

S.B.

BACK LANE

S.P

BACK LANE

HORSELOW STREET

Goods Shed

W.M

Baptist Chapel

B.Gd

Cattle Pens

S.B.

Potter's Charity

F.B.

CHAPEL YARD

Station

Meth. Church

Tk.

School

BACK STREET

Red Lion Inn

Schools

STATION ROAD

OAK CRESCENT

OAK CRESCENT

G.P.

L.B

MOON'S CORNER

P.H.

BLACKBIRD STREET

ROAD

85.   An Edwardian postcard shows a packed goods yard and a Cambridge-bound train. No. 1 Box is on the right and No. 2 is in the distance. (Lens of Sutton coll.)

86.   The goods yard closed on 1st January 1966 and this is one of the last trains. The locomotive is BR class 4 4-6-0 no. 75028. The Sandy & Potton Steam Railway Association was formed in 1969, but it was not successful in raising sufficient funds to proceed. (G.Howe)

87.	A DMU bound for Cambridge was recorded from the cattle dock line in 1965. Blue paving bricks and gas lighting lasted to the end. (G.Howe)

88.	The down side shelter was still intact when diesel shunter no. D3689 was photographed running in with the demolition train in 1969. There had been a large water tank on a brick base in the right foreground. (G.Howe)

89.	A	1990 photograph reveals that the historic building had been tastefully conserved, but a meat factory was built in the background. The arches on the right were windows in the rear wall of the water tower. There was a steam pump for raising water from a well under the tower. (A.C.Mott)

GAMLINGAY

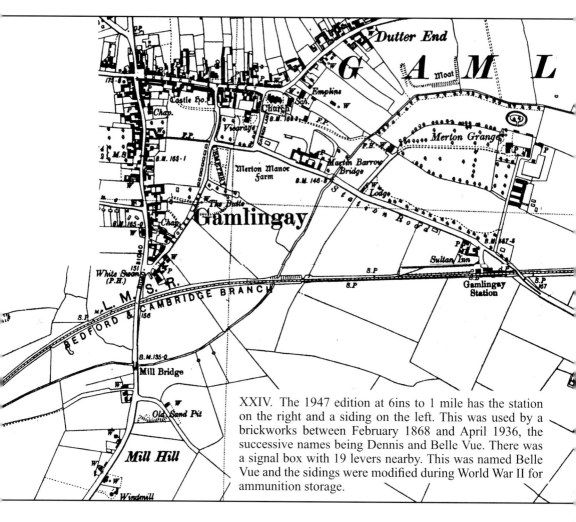

XXIV. The 1947 edition at 6ins to 1 mile has the station on the right and a siding on the left. This was used by a brickworks between February 1868 and April 1936, the successive names being Dennis and Belle Vue. There was a signal box with 19 levers nearby. This was named Belle Vue and the sidings were modified during World War II for ammunition storage.

XXV. The 1900 revision shows a layout which changed little. The station served 1722 folk in 1901 and 1622 in 1961.

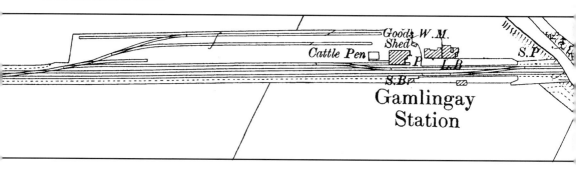

90. The lack of a footbridge is evident again in this eastward view from an Edwardian postcard. The crossover was one of two used normally during freight movements. (Lens of Sutton)

91. Four photographs from 24th May 1957 give a comprehensive survey of the substantial buildings, with their fine chimneys and stacks. The letter box and one mailbag are evident, as is the shed road buffer stop. (R.M.Casserley)

92.   Most of the goods yard is visible, as is the goods office. Freight facilities were withdrawn on 10th April 1965. The signal box had 18 levers, only 9 of which were used. (R.M.Casserley)

93.   The prospective passenger's perspective is presented in this inevitably dull record of the north elevation. Note the inset arches over certain windows. (R.M.Casserley)

94.   Rods did not run to the far end of the goods yard; instead there was a ground frame, which could be unlocked by an Annetts key. Oil lamps remained to the end. (R.M.Casserley)

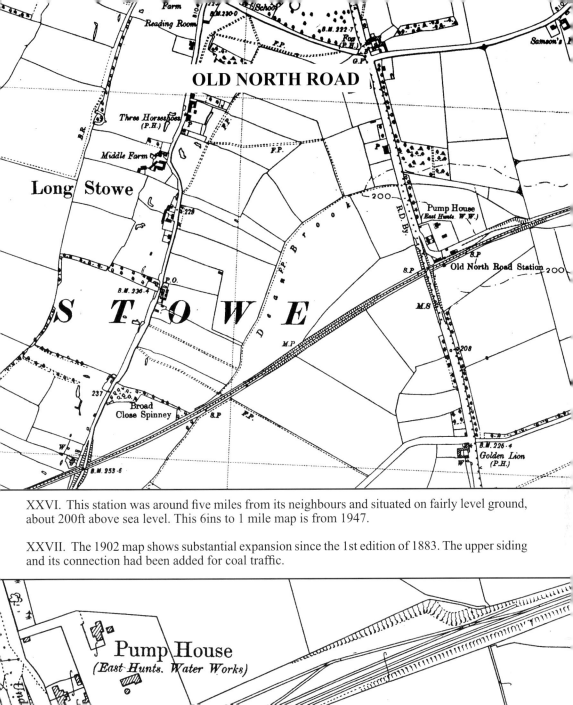

OLD NORTH ROAD

Long Stowe

S · T · O · W · E

Three Horseshoes (P.H.)

Middle Farm

Reading Room

Fox (P.H.)

Samson's

Pump House (East Hunts. W.W.)

Old North Road Station

Broad Close Spinney

Golden Lion (P.H.)

XXVI. This station was around five miles from its neighbours and situated on fairly level ground, about 200ft above sea level. This 6ins to 1 mile map is from 1947.

XXVII. The 1902 map shows substantial expansion since the 1st edition of 1883. The upper siding and its connection had been added for coal traffic.

Pump House
(East Hunts. Water Works)

Cattle Pen

Goods Shed

Old North Road
Station

95.   A late Victorian view is suggested as the stationmaster appears to have a frock coat and the final signal box has not yet been built. The other staff are probably signalman, porter and clerk. The first box was on the up platform, level with the cattle pen. The building on the right is probably the second box. (Lens of Sutton)

96.   Class 4F 0-6-0 no. 4511 was one of a batch of 580 such locomotives begun in 1924 and was probably photographed in the 1930s. The signal box was built near the platform edge for good visibility. (Lens of Sutton coll.)

97.   The north elevation makes an interesting comparison with the neighbour at Gamlingay (picture 93), as it is reversed and has a TELEPHONE sign. You paid the booking clerk after the operator had timed the call and declared the cost. (H.C.Casserley)

98.   A second photograph from 28th September 1957 and this features ex-LNER class B1 4-6-0 no. 61052 with a long eastbound goods train of the type for which the Bletchley flyover was intended. The goods yard closed on 19th April 1965. (H.C.Casserley)

99.   The bridge carried the A14 so numbered in 1919; it is now the A1198. In Roman times it had been Ermine Street. The structure was replaced with concrete beams a few years before closure. Toft & Kingston Sidings were further east and they were in use for agricultural traffic between 1911 and 1951. (R.M.Casserley)

100.   The signal box had 15 levers and was in use until the last day of 1967. The new bridge is seen from the rear of a DMU on 30th July 1966. (R.Hummerston)

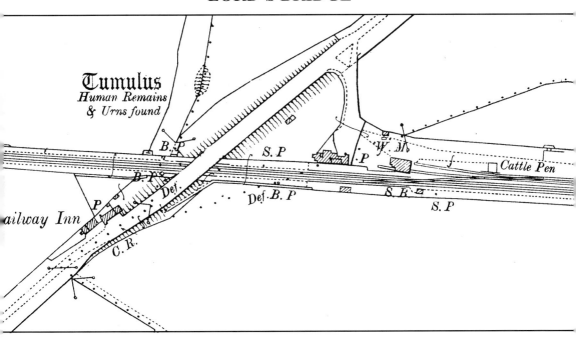

XXVIII. The 1902 edition shows a layout which remained unchanged to the end, apart from the addition of sidings south of the station for the RAF Ammunition Depot. Mustard gas shells were also filled here until a massive explosion and fire took place on 11th January 1955.

101.   Snow clearance was an unusual subject for a photographer back in 1902. The small signal box had a 15-lever frame. (Lens of Sutton)

102.   A "Precursor" class 4-4-0 waits to depart west, in about the 1920s. This type was introduced in 1904. The panorama is from the A603 bridge. (Lens of Sutton)

103.   The buildings were similar to those at the two stations to the west, already seen. All the goods sheds had 25cwt cranes and such traffic ceased on 13th July 1964. This and the next photograph are from 28th September 1957. (R.M.Casserley)

104.   The 1934 Hillman 10 served the photographer until MOTs were invented in 1960 - say no more! The flat-roofed section (left) housed the water tank and facilities for gentlemen, hence the ventilators. (H.C.Casserley)

105.   The buildings, together with much of the RAF Depot, became part of the Mullard Radio Astronomy Observatory of Cambridge University. Two telescopes ran on about ½ mile of 20ft gauge track on the old railway route and are seen in 2003. (Nick Catford)

106.   Ex-LNWR "Cauliflower" class 0-6-0 no. 8439 is running from Cambridge to Bletchley near Trumpington. The fixed distant warns of Cambridge Goods Yard box, the last on the LMS route and rebuilt in 1944. (P.Q.Treloar coll.)

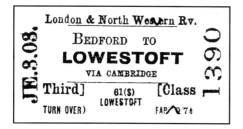

London & North Western Ry.

BEDFORD TO
LOWESTOFT
VIA CAMBRIDGE

Third]   61(S)   [Class
             LOWESTOFT
TURN OVER)   FAP/2 '74

JE.8.08.   1390

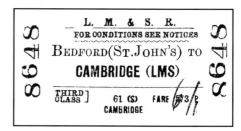

L. M. & S. R.
FOR CONDITIONS SEE NOTICES

BEDFORD(ST.JOHN'S) TO
CAMBRIDGE (LMS)

THIRD]   61 (S)   FARE 5/3/P
CLASS   CAMBRIDGE

8648   8648

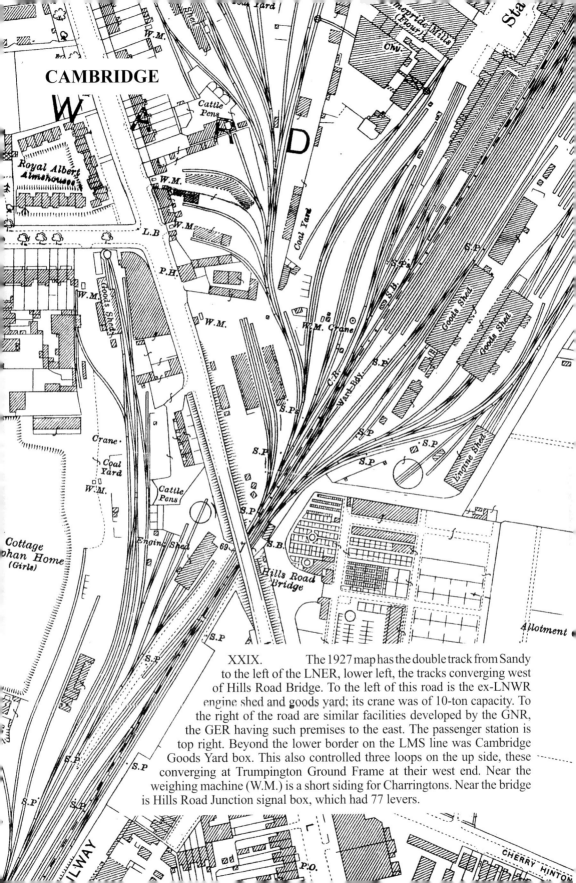

CAMBRIDGE

Royal Albert Almshouses

Cottage Orphan Home (Girls)

Cattle Pens

Coal Yard

Goods Shed

Goods Shed

Goods Shed

Engine Shed

Crane

Coal Yard

Cattle Pens

Engine Shed

Hills Road Bridge

Allotment

CHERRY HINTON

RAILWAY

XXIX.   The 1927 map has the double track from Sandy to the left of the LNER, lower left, the tracks converging west of Hills Road Bridge. To the left of this road is the ex-LNWR engine shed and goods yard; its crane was of 10-ton capacity. To the right of the road are similar facilities developed by the GNR, the GER having such premises to the east. The passenger station is top right. Beyond the lower border on the LMS line was Cambridge Goods Yard box. This also controlled three loops on the up side, these converging at Trumpington Ground Frame at their west end. Near the weighing machine (W.M.) is a short siding for Charringtons. Near the bridge is Hills Road Junction signal box, which had 77 levers.

107.   The station opened on 30th July 1845 and the heraldic devices of the Cambridge University colleges were incorporated between the arches. The GNR had a separate building to the south of this one, behind the right border of this picture. (Lens of Sutton coll.)

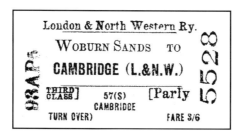

108.   Through trains still use opposite ends of one long platform, which is divided by a scissors crossover. This applied from 16th November 1863, when the up platform and subway were removed. There were several attempts in the 1880s to have them replaced on safety grounds. (Lens of Sutton coll.)

109.   Nicknamed *Tishy* after a racehorse, LMS 4-6-0 no. 25845 was one of four of its class to have inside cylinders, but outside Walschaerts valve gear. Part of the former GNR depot is on the left and the flour mills are on the right. (A.G.W.Garraway)

110. Two bay platforms were provided at both ends of the station, the southern ones being used for GNR and LNWR services. The western one accommodates the 7.03am from Bletchley after arrival on 20th May 1938. The former GNR building is behind it. (H.C.Casserley)

111. Seen on the same day in the adjacent yard is LMS "Prince of Wales" class 4-6-0 no. 25722. Also included are early examples of containerisation, plus part of Sadler's massive Home Pride flour mills. Idle in 2006, they awaited conversion to apartments, formerly known as flats. (H.C.Casserley)

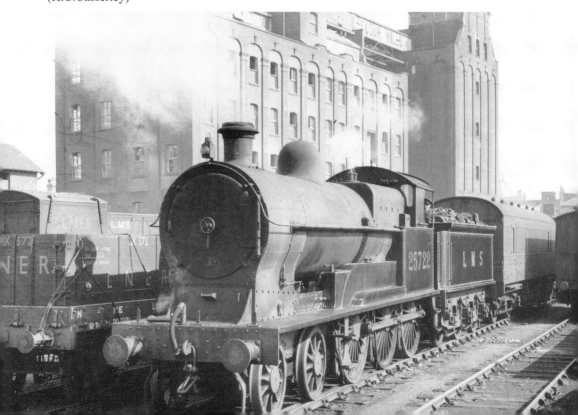

112.   A southward panorama from Hills Road on 5th September 1959 has BR class 4 2-6-4T no. 80084 with a train from Bletchley at the eastern end of that route. On the right is part of the former LNWR goods yard, plus the water column outside its engine shed. (S.Rickard/J&J coll.)

113.   The engine shed had closed in October 1935 and the final Cambridge goods yard succumbed in 1971. The turntable is obscured by the shed; the ex-LNWR yard was to the left. (R.M.Casserley)

114. A train to Bletchley stands behind BR class 4MT 4-6-0 no. 75038 on 15th August 1959. Part of the GNR building can be seen above the second coach. It still stands, but has not been used by passengers for generations. (F.Hornby)

115.   South Box is in this view from 5th September 1959 as a DMU is about to pass under Hills Road, bound for Colchester. The jib of the 10-ton crane in the former GNR goods yard is visible. (S.Rickard/J&J coll.)

116.   A rail event was held on 29th September 1990 in the carriage sidings adjacent to platform 3. Diesel shunter no. 08631 is hauling a DMU which is attached to Hudswell Clarke 0-6-0T *Thomas* from the Nene Valley Railway. It will return after a brief trip on part of the route once used by trains to Bedford. (P.G.Barnes)

Other albums to feature this station -
Branch Lines around Huntington
Cambridge to Ely
Potters Bar to Cambridge

117. The remaining LNWR yard track, including that in the former Charrington's depot, was donated (courtesy of Railtrack and Cambridge University Press) to the Mid-Norfolk Railway and was dismantled by them during the summer of 1999. Most was removed by a series of four trains hired from EWS, each of which worked onto the line to be loaded on site. Although disused for some time, and overgrown, it was deemed fit for use with vegetation clearance taking place prior to the arrival of the first train. All reclaimed materials were transported to Dereham. (R.Hummerston)

118.   The final train left on 24th August 1999 when no. ➡️
58037 came onto the line to take loaded wagons over to the
sidings opposite Cambridge station. Thereafter, because of
the short length of track left, it and other materials remaining
on site were taken to Dereham by road. Thus the last evidence
of the LNWR in Cambridge was removed. Hills Road bridge
is in the background. (R.Hummerston)

119.   The building used by the
GNR was largely intact when its
west facade was recorded on 7th
January 2006. The structure was
used for offices and buffet stores at
that time. (V.Mitchell)

➡️
120.   The east elevation was photographed on the same day during one of the brief spells when
platforms 2 and 3 were both vacated. Originally GNR trains used the one nearest their building
and LNWR services frequented the one on the right, but there was no distinction in the latter years
of steam. Now electrified, they are busy with local trains to London on two routes. (V.Mitchell)

MP Middleton Press

Easebourne Lane, Midhurst, West Sussex.
GU29 9AZ   Tel:01730 813169

EVOLVING THE ULTIMATE RAIL ENCYCLOPEDIA

www.middletonpress.co.uk   email:info@middletonpress.co.uk
A-0 906520   B-1 873793   C-1 901706   D-1 904474

OOP Out of print at time of printing - Please check availability   BROCHURE AVAILABLE SHOWING NEW TITLES